Lust, Love, and Breakups

Written by Melissa Edmunds
with Assistance by Cindy Bruce

Copyright. 2013

ISBN: 978-1-300-74996-7

CONTENTS

BREAK UP
(Written by Cindy Bruce)

I know she's in love with you
I know that you're going to make her happy.
I know you have moved on and I have to.
I just wanted to be friends.

I want you to know that you hurt me.
You really really hurt me.
You broke my heart.
The same as I broke yours,
but we have to move forward.
Live our lives a part as lovers
and still be best friends.

SHE LIES
(Written by: Cindy Bruce)

Truth is too hard to handle so I let her lie.
She said she wouldn't do it again .
The day I left she was asleep on the sofa and I let her lay.
Why should I be with someone when I let her lie.

She is always in my heart
and I can't figure out why she's in my world
I wonder why I let her treat me this way
when I let her lie.

TEAR ON MY PILLOW

When I lay and think, in my bed at night,

the day you'll arrive, seems nowhere in sight.

I toss and I turn, dreaming of you.

Opening my eyes.... checking if my dream came true.

It didn't, again, and a tear starts to roll,

weeping quietly... my pillow I hold.

Many sleepless nights I've prayed for you, my love.

THE DAY

The day you came into my life

everything changed,

you brought happiness,

you brought hope,

you brought contentment.

And most of all,

you brought love,

a love so amazing,

a love so powerful,

a love too beautiful

to ever be defined.

The day you came into my life

you gave me everything,

and I'll love you always.

THE ONLY ONE

When I think of the things I love about you
my heart fills with a joy
that would take a lietime to consume.

Your eyes, your touch,
your smile, your hugs,
your laughter, your walk,
the sound of your voice whenever you talk.

Your worries, your fears,
your desires, your dreams,
everything about you mesmerizes me.

My wish is to make you smile
to make you happy
to make all your dreams come true.

Because my heart knows
you're the only one for me.

THESE ARMS

With these arms, I've held you close,

stroked your ace, and wiped your teary eyes.

With these arms, I've induced ectasy and

sheer bliss.

With these arms, I've made you smile, even

laugh hsterically.

With these arms, I shall hold yours forever.

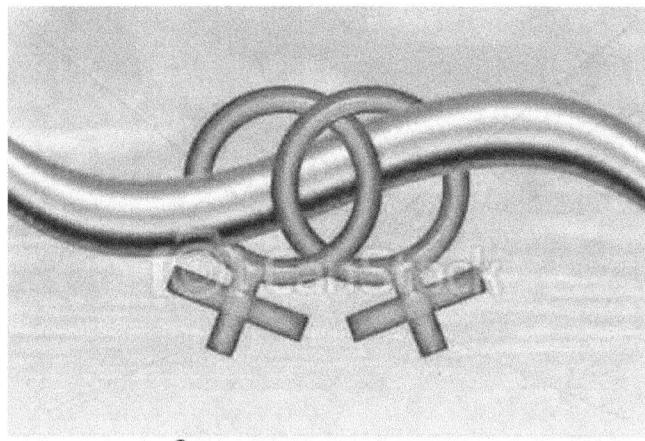

THINKING OF YOU
(Written with Cindy Bruce)

While sitting alone with nothing to do
my mind becomes filled with thoughts of you.

The sun goes down, the moon comes up
and the stars come out to play.

Things I could have said, the things I sould have done
the expression of words that make two as one.

I lay on a blanket and watch for shooting stars to fall
so I can make a wish, to stay together with you foreveremore.

Photographs strewn on the floor, eyes well up
night and day goes by, all I think about is you.

THIS HEART

If you said you were cold,

I would wrap my arms around you.

If you said you were thirsty,

I would give you the ocean.

I would give you anything

the moon, the start, the sunset too.

This heart in my hands

I hold out to you.

THOUGHTS OF YOU
(Written with Cindy Bruce)

As I sit here
staring at a picture of you,
my mind wonders to
a love that is true.

You hair is so blonde
your eyes are so blue,
that is what attracted me to you,
that is why your heart is so true.

My heart beats loud
your stare is so true,
your body moves like the wind
and my mind's always on you.

When I'm in the shower
or laying in bed,
I always see a picture
of you in my head.

TO BE WITH YOU

I sit here in the night
staring into the Heavens above.
Wondering if I'm lucky enough
to be given your love.

Even thought I met you
not that long aga.
I have learned so much of who yo are
and thirst to learn more.

I want to share my world with you,
all the smiles and all the tears.
I want to learn to trust again,
something I haven't done in years.

You are very special to me,
you have kindled something new.
I want to feel loved in life,
I want to be with you.

TO LOVE

As fas as the ocean is wide
through miles and miles of sea,
you will be someone special
a true miracle to me.

As high upon the mountain tops
as high as one can climb,
you will be so dear to me
the best friend I can find.

As many stars that twinkle
thoughout the Heavens above,
you will be a bright reminder
of what it means to love.

TOUCH

Your touch...
No words can explain only with the expression mmmmm... remains

Your touch...
Gives me an adrenaline rush high on cloud 9 from your love makes me blush
can never get enough

Your touch...
Induced me into erotic bliss mmmmmm... love your lips and the way they kiss
makes me tingle down to my finger tips

Your touch...
Leaves me breathing hard but shallow as you kiss my neck
your hands ollow the motion of my hips and
explore the rest of my body your tongue dances on my skin with each kiss
no other woman can fulfill me with orgasmic bliss

Your touch...
Physical pleasures I treasure for you are the one and only
who satisies me to that measure of magnitude having a constant craving
yearning for your touch....

TRUST

Trust
before the mirror
no clear reflection
I flirt with fear
dodging rejection
eyes of a judge
stare back at me
I won't budge
the truth they see
for who if not me
knows of my shame
when only I see
where lies the blame
so, what did I do?
For what shall I pay?
Or should I eschew
the price of this day
but if I'm to grow
then measure I must
it's then I will know
if it's me that I trust.

WAITING FOR YOU

If rough winds blow you miles away
or whirling waves lead you astray,
I won't forget your last goodbye
you know I'll be waiting for you.

If hardships strain you to that land
and lie gets too tough to withstand
you'll conquer all with love so true
to know someone's waiting for you.

When you lose faith in all that's pure
and doubt things of which you were sure
whenever you don't have a clue
remember I'm waiting for you.

I days and months and years pass by
even if the ocean runs dry
I'll see the day when we'll be two
and 'til that day I'll wait for you.

WAITING TO BE LOVED

You hide behind your feeling
and keep the truth locked away,
but there is so much said
in the things you don't say.

You innocently tell me
our time has come and gone
and that we can't go back
but I don't believe it
and this time your wrong.

The distance you put between us
is nothing more than time lost,
a place for your feelings to hide
yet I can hear the love in your voice
each time we talk.

My patience has no end
when it comes to loving you
and I will wait a lietime
for you to see the truth.

Real love doesn't go away
if doesn't fade into the past,
it goes on forever
and always finds its way back.

I will wait a lifetime for you
because you are my soul,
and behind all of your doubt
I know you can't let go.

You are my soul
and I am yours too,
if two people were ever
meant to be,
it's you and me!!

WAITING

No one else
compare to you,
I honestly thought
we were stuck like glue.

Then you decided
you needed a break,
with you my heart
I allowed you to take.

I broke down and cryed
searched my skin,
for some sort of wound
where the pain did begin.

I didn't know what to do
I ran away,
I couldn't stop thinking
of things I didn't say.

I said I would wait
wait for you to decide,
maybe it would be enough
for the pain to subside.

How long will it take
what if I'm forgoten,
left out in the rain
my heart molded and rotten?

Is a life spent waiting
truely a life at all,
waiting by the phone
dying for a call?

Ia a life without you
one I wish to l ive,
how could I find another,
if I don't have a heart to give?

I can't take it back
or rather I won't,

people said I'd want another
honestly I don't.

WHAT I CRAVE

I wonder....
if its all really worth it
the tears, the hurt,
the smiles, the laughs.

I'd be better off alone
I was made to be used
I don't need to feel this way
my mind consumed.

Fuck me like you hate me
show me how to ride
spank me like you mean it
fucking look me in the eyes.

Use me
abuse me
please give me what I crave.

WHAT IT MEANS TO LOVE

As far as the ocean is wide
through miles and miles of sea,
you will be someone special
a true miracle to me.

As high upon the mountaintops
as high as one can climb,
you will be so dear to me
the best friend I can find.

As many stars that twinkle
throughout the heavens above,
you will be a bright reminder
of what if means to love.

WHERE YOU ARE

From where you are
you have the power to touch my heart
you've reached a place deep inside
no one else could ever find.

You've turned my world around
and I'm so lost in you now
that even if I wanted to
I can't be found.

From where you are
you move me in so many ways
lift my spirits, take my breath away
and I can feel the love
without the simplicity of one touch.

From where I stand
I can see all that I am
where you are.

WITHOUT YOU

You're the blood in my viens

that keeps me alive

you're the cool air

that I breath during the night

you're the burning flame

that mkes me see through the dark

you're the straight path

that I'm trudging on when my days turn bad.

Safety is what I sought within your arms

kisses that brought tingling deep down

passion we shared so intense I can't deny

I dunno what I'll do without you in my life.

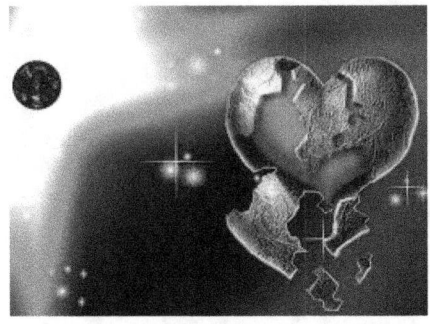

WITHOUT YOU

You're always on my mind, day and night

when I think of you, all feels so right

need to have you, need to hold you

and tell you that I love you.

My dear, I don't want to see us apart

this separation just tears away my heart

I miss you, oh, I really miss you

will need you more and more each day

I know I cannot live without you

I miss you, more than words can say.

WRONG
(Written by: Cindy Bruce)

As I sit and drive down the road
I could work a couple months ago
you were here by my side
I don't know what happened
I don't know what went wrong.
I have time to Think as I drive a long
and you not by my side.
It's quiet in the car
no one to talk to because my daughter is asleep.
I have time to think because
there's nothing else to do
but think of what I did wrong.

YOU AND I

You make me feel special
you make me feel new,
you make me feel loved
with everything you do.

You hold me close when I am sad
you wipe the tears from my face,
everytime we are together
it seems like the perfect place.

My eyes light up when you enter a room
I smile when we are together,
no matter how bad things are
you always make them better.

I love the way you kiss me
the way you hold me tight,
I love the way you touch me
I could be with you all night.

I love the way you can make me laugh
for absolutely no reason at all.
I love how no matter what I do
you will be there to catch me when I fall.

I just want you to know
that even though we sometimes fight,
I will always love you
no matter what.

YOU TURNED

No one can see
the hurt that is inside of me,
or the shell of the person
that I have come to be.

I'm dieing inside
and no one seems to care,
I wish the pain would stop
and the end was near.

I used to be happy
and filled with love,
but it all went away
when you turned your back that day.

YOU WINK, YOU SMILE

I take you first
where you like it best.

Right on the lips
I nibble and kiss
a venusian mound.

A hood,
a flower,
I'm down for an hour.

Patiently sucking
between active thighs,
all as I capture
the moon
in your eyes.

ditching your waist
my hands go for yours,
enticing them
wanting them
to follow me back down.

The find a home at
the back of my head.
            Yes,
I will have the
first triumph tonight.

Where you like it best
in summer moonlight.

Thrusting your hips,
arching your back,
you melt on my face
like hot candle wax.

Then,
butterfly kisses,
up and down slow.
A second peak bliss,
a river-like flow.

You wink, you smile.
Content and serene.

YOU WON'T FORGET

Remove your knickers with my teeth pretty pussy needs relief
slowly starting at your feet soon you'll feel my sexual heat
licking legs stroking thighs my cunt is wet my clitoris rise
lick you softly behind your knees brush your bottom lightly tease
I won't touch your fanny yet even though you're streaming wet
rhythmically my hands roaming see your yoni now is foaming
moan and writhe you little bitch I'll make you beg me scratch your itch.

Lie on top begin to shunt now we're lying cunt to cunt
you arch your back offer your crack this night no pleasure whall we lack
still I work and watch you jerk no release 'til you go berserk
kiss you now caress inner thighs you arch even higher to offer your prize.

No way baby!

You ain't really suffered yet I'll make your pleasure hard to get
my finger running around your rim wet it first then slip it in
your moaning groaning wanting more slip off the bed onto the floor
spread your buttocks tongue in cheek you're getting near now start to shriek.

finished now with your copper pit now I'm easing up a bit
two fingers in your honey pot God it feels so bloody hot.

Then I sit upon your face let you taste my holy place
I cum in gushes make you drink beside yourself you're on the brink
you push my head between your legs "Oh please,Oh please" I hear you beg
with lightest flicks on your hard clit cum juices shooting from your slit
screams of wild abandoned joy you never got with anyone
back in bed fondling breast I kiss you tell you you're the best
I'll give you a night you won't forget.

YOUR BODY MOVES

I close my eyes
thinking about you,
my hands touching your skin
slowly turning you on.

My kissess on your soft silky skin
as I enjoy the feeling inside that you have caused
kissing my way doen,
your pussy throbbing.

You open your legs allowing me to have my way with you,
as you feel my kisses on your thigh, then you pussy,
as my tongue
slips inside.

You moan as I move my tongue in and out,
I feel you cum
as I slide my fingers
thrusting as you continue to moan.

Your moans fill the room,
as I suck on your clit
making you feel like you're climbing the wall
as you cum again.

Your body moves under me
and you grab me
pulling me in
wanting more.

You cum and cum over and over
your body trembles,
as the last orgasm escapes
you call out my name.

YOUR HAND

I haven't forgotten
taht I am just one person,
that I am but one voice
attempting to stand out
from the crowd.

I remember
that I have fallen
amidst the laughter
that surrounds me, and that sometimes
it gets too loud.

I know that I can't sit here
and expect my silence
to evoke change
without reason.

I can see
taht I don't know everything,
that I can't expect
my hand to be held
always.

I can feel
that time is slipping
by me, that it
will be gone if I just
stand still.

I have heard
that there are a million
other voices that sound
like mine, that want also
to be heard.

I've been told
that it's not enough to
wish for dreams, that I
have to work them
into reality.

I know that I don't know

all that I think I know.
I know I won't see all of
the places I wish to go.
I know I'm not ready
for all that the world demands,
you don't have to always hold me,
just let me see your hands.

I know
that there's a lot
that I won't understand,
that you don't have all
of the answers.

I haven't forgotten
that I have to grow up
and someda live without
your voice, your opinion - -
making my own decisions.

I know that I don't know
all that I think I know.
I know that I may not see all
of the places I want to someday go.
I know I'm not ready for everything
that I won't always understand
you don't have to always hold me
but sometimes.....
Just let me touch your
hand!

YOUR SMILE

When the day has been long
and the troubles last into the night,
all you've gotta do is smile
and everything is suddenly alright.

When I feel the weight of the world
upon my shoulders
and let things get under my skin,
all you've gotta do is smile
and I'm ready to try once again.

When words or actions of another bring me down
or if I'm feeling pretty low,
all you've gotta do is smile
and I know I'm not alone.

When I'm hard on myself
and find it difficult to believe in me
all you've gotta do is smile
and I know I can accomplish anything.

Your smile does so many things
it brightens up my day,
your smile is like a promise
that things will be okay.

Your smile is all I really need
to ease fear, disappointment or doubt,
your smile lightens my heart
and it's something I never want to be without.

YOUR WORDS

Your words in whispers excite my heart
fill my mind with passion unexplored.
Your soft lips seduce as they linger where pressed.
My body now longing, begging for more.

The touch of your hands as they wonder
sends chills racing deep within.
The heat of your body close so close to mine
is sweet pleasure indulging my skin.

Desires over whelm me, yet I can't get enough
I crave everything that is you.
I get lost in your eyes, and am swept away
by each sultry, hypnotizing move.

Meliss Edmunds

I have numerous poems published. I was born and raised in Wyoming. I enjoy writing and have been doing so most of my life. I got a lot of inspiration from my brother, who is dearly missed. I hope you enjoy, thank you.